the
life
of
christ

a pictorial essay from the living bible

TYNDALE HOUSE PUBLISHERS
Wheaton, Illinois
COVERDALE HOUSE PUBLISHERS
London, England

Photography by Alan (Wim) Auceps, except pho-
tographs of actual Bibleland scenes courtesy of the
Israel Ministry of Tourism.

Design: Gardner Hutchins

All the text of *The Life of Christ* is from *The
Living Bible*, © 1971 by Tyndale House Publishers,
Wheaton, Illinois, and is used by permission.

The Life of Christ. Library of Congress Catalog
Card Number 73-92956; ISBN 8423-2215-9. Copy-
right © 1974 Tyndale House Publishers, Inc.,
Wheaton, Illinois. All rights reserved. Second print-
ing, April 1974. Printed in the U.S.A.

The Life of Christ, a pictorial essay, is a unique combination of the accomplishments of Kenneth N. Taylor, Wheaton, Illinois and Wim Auceps, Paris, France.

Fresh, youthful, living photography combines with Scripture passages from the easy-to-read *Living Bible* to provide a rare and inspiring adventure.

On the eve of the publication of *The Living Bible* in sixteen European languages (along with some 100 other languages throughout the world), this book heralds a new era of international understanding and appreciation of the gospel of Jesus Christ.

About the photographer, Wim Auceps

Wim Auceps was born of Communist parents and raised in the slums of pre-war Amsterdam, Holland. Conversion to Christianity changed his outlook on the nature and needs of man, giving him profound sensitivity, understanding and perspective.

His faith unshaken by the atrocities of World War II, Auceps' conviction that he should serve Christ led him first to seminary training at Institut Biblique Europeen in Lamorlaye, France, and then into active youth work in France.

Auceps' work with young people centered around a summer camp ministry. A typical summer found him with forty or fifty teen-agers in the Bibleland-like atmosphere of southwestern France . . . using his campers to portray Bible characters in multi-projector 35 mm audio-visual presentations. A local seamstress helped design and create a wardrobe of Bible era costumes. From day to day Auceps and his crew of young "stars" and "extras" went out "on location" to the hills, the seashore, the quaint villages and even into the picturesque old city of Marseilles, filming sequences from the Bible.

The results are presented in this book. We believe you will appreciate its unique, unsophisticated presentation of the ministry and life of Jesus Christ.

Dr. Kenneth N. Taylor's paraphrasing of *The Living Bible* was initially undertaken for the enjoyment and instruction of his ten children. On weekday mornings, as he rode the commuter train to his Chicago office, Taylor spent his time rewriting passages first from St. Paul's Epistle to the Romans, and later from the other letters to the early churches, into a modern-day English that his children could easily understand and appreciate.

The interest and encouragement of his family and friends led him to found Tyndale House Publishers in 1962 for the publication of these paraphrased epistles in book form, entitled *Living Letters*. The success of this first book led to publication of another paraphrased portion of the Bible, *Living Prophecies*, and to another, *Living Gospels*, and to yet others, until in 1971 *The Living Bible* was produced in a one-volume edition, climaxing fourteen years of intensive study and writing.

The success story of *The Living Bible* is publishing history. Within two years after the first copies were placed on the market, more than ten million copies were produced and sold, outselling the most phenomenal of best-sellers.

Before anything else existed,
there was Christ, with God.
Eternal life is in him,
and this life gives light
to all mankind.

When the right time came, the time God decided on, he sent his Son, born of a woman, born as a Jew, to buy freedom for us who were slaves to the law so that he could adopt us as his very own sons. And Christ became a human being and lived here on earth among us and was full of loving forgiveness and truth.

To give light to those who sit in darkness and death's shadow, and to guide us to the path of peace. He will bring true justice and peace to all the nations of the world.

*t*hese are the facts concerning the birth of Jesus Christ:

God sent the angel Gabriel to Nazareth, a village in Galilee, to a virgin, Mary, engaged to be married to a man named Joseph, a descendant of King David. Gabriel appeared to her and said, "Congratulations, favored lady! The Lord is with you!" Confused and disturbed, Mary tried to think what the angel could mean.

"Don't be frightened, Mary," the angel told her, "for God has decided to wonderfully bless you! Very soon now, you will become pregnant and have a baby boy, and you are to name him 'Jesus.' He shall be very great and shall be called the Son of God. And the Lord God shall give him the throne of his ancestor David. And he shall reign over Israel forever; his Kingdom shall never end!"

These will be his royal titles: Wonderful, Counselor, The Mighty God, The Everlasting Father, The Prince of Peace.

*M*ary asked the angel, "But how can I have a baby? I am a virgin."

The angel replied, "The Holy Spirit shall come upon you, and the power of God shall overshadow you; so the baby born to you will be utterly holy —the Son of God."

Mary said, "I am the Lord's servant, and I am willing to do whatever he wants. May everything you said come true. . . . Oh, how I praise the Lord. How I rejoice in God my Savior! For he took notice of his lowly servant girl, and now generation after generation forever shall call me blest of God. For he, the mighty Holy One, has done great things to me. His mercy goes on from generation to generation, to all who reverence him."

While she was still a virgin Mary became pregnant by the Holy Spirit. Then Joseph, her fiancé, being a man of stern principle, decided to break the engagement but to do it quietly, as he didn't want to publicly disgrace her.

As he lay awake considering this, he fell into a dream, and saw an angel standing beside him. "Joseph, son of David," the angel said, "don't hesitate to take Mary as your wife! For the child within her has been conceived by the Holy Spirit. And she will have a Son, and you shall name him Jesus (meaning 'Savior'), for he will save his people from their sins."

Caesar Augustus, the Roman Emperor, decreed that a census should be taken throughout the nation. Everyone was required to return to his ancestral home for this registration. And because Joseph was a member of the royal line, he had to go to Bethlehem in Judea, King David's ancient home—journeying there from the Galilean village of Nazareth. He took with him Mary, his fiancée, who was obviously pregnant by this time.

O Bethlehem Ephrathah,
you are but a small Judean village,
yet you will be the birthplace
of my King who is alive
from everlasting ages past.

And while they were there, the time came for her baby to be born; and she gave birth to her first child, a son. She wrapped him in a blanket and laid him in a manger, because there was no room for them in the village inn.

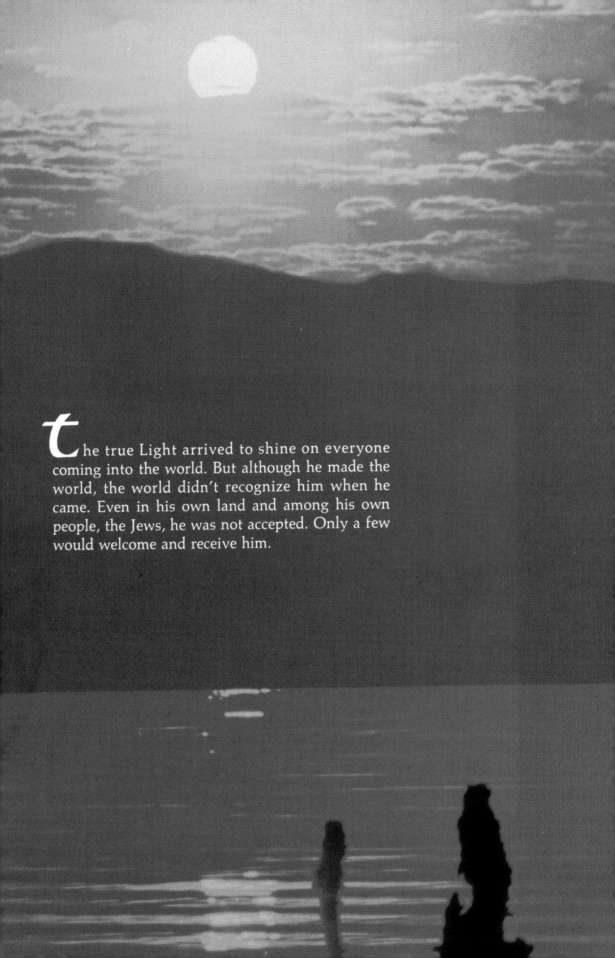

*t*he true Light arrived to shine on everyone coming into the world. But although he made the world, the world didn't recognize him when he came. Even in his own land and among his own people, the Jews, he was not accepted. Only a few would welcome and receive him.

*t*hat night some shepherds were in the fields outside the village, guarding their flocks of sheep. Suddenly an angel appeared among them, and the landscape shone bright with the glory of the Lord. They were badly frightened, but the angel reassured them.

"Don't be afraid!" he said. "I bring you the most joyful news ever announced, and it is for everyone! The Savior—yes, the Messiah, the Lord—has been born tonight in Bethlehem!"

Suddenly, the angel was joined by a vast host of others—the armies of heaven—praising God: "Glory to God in the highest heaven," they sang, "and peace on earth for all those pleasing him."

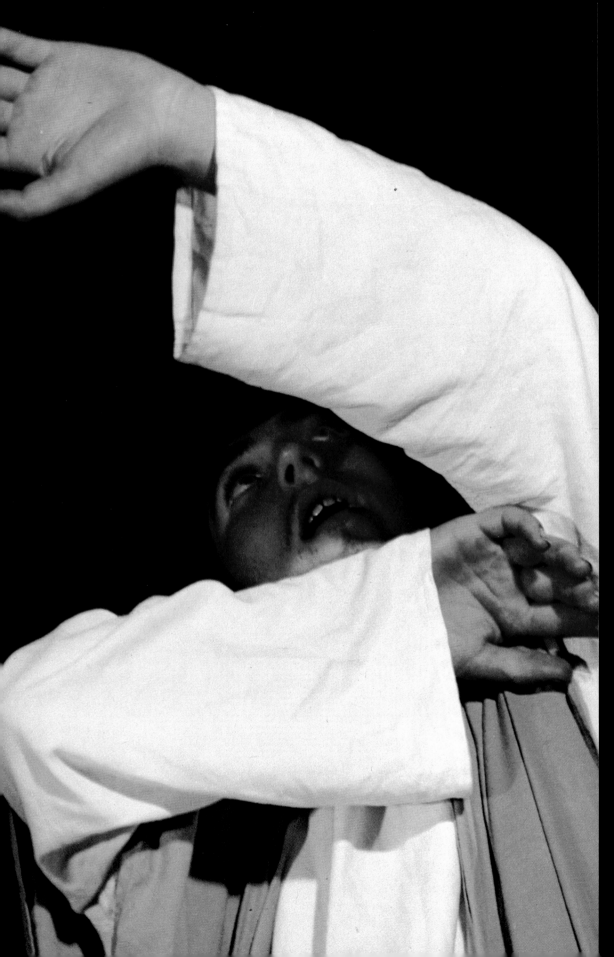

When this great army of angels had returned again to heaven, the shepherds said to each other, "Come on! Let's go to Bethlehem! Let's see this wonderful thing that has happened, which the Lord has told us about." They ran to the village and found their way to Mary and Joseph.

Shout with joy before the Lord, O earth! Obey him gladly; come before him, singing with joy. Go through his open gates with great thanksgiving; enter his courts with praise. Give thanks to him and bless his name.

Merchants from around the world will flow to you, bringing you the wealth of many lands. Vast droves of camels will converge upon you . . . bringing gold and incense to add to the praise of God. All will bring their gifts. Yes, kings from everywhere! All will bow before him! All will serve him! Let him reign from sea to sea.

astrologers from eastern lands arrived in Jerusalem, asking, "Where is the newborn King of the Jews? for we have seen his star in far-off eastern lands, and have come to worship him."

King Herod was deeply disturbed by their question, and all Jerusalem was filled with rumors. He called a meeting of all the Jewish religious leaders.

"Did the prophets tell us where the Messiah would be born?" he asked.

"Yes, in Bethlehem," they said, "for this is what the prophet Micah wrote:

"'O little town of Bethlehem, you are not just an unimportant Judean village, for a Governor shall rise from you to rule my people Israel.'"

*t*hen Herod sent a private message to the astrologers, asking them to come to see him; at this meeting he found out from them the exact time when they first saw the star. Then he told them, "Go to Bethlehem and search for the child. And when you find him, come back and tell me so that I can go and worship him too!"

*a*fter this interview the astrologers started out again. And look! The star appeared to them again, standing over Bethlehem. Their joy knew no bounds! Entering the house where the baby and Mary his mother were, they threw themselves down before him, worshiping. Then they opened their presents and gave him gold, frankincense and myrrh.

But when they returned to their own land, they didn't go through Jerusalem to report to Herod, for God had warned them in a dream to go home another way.

After they were gone, an angel of the Lord appeared to Joseph in a dream. "Get up and flee to Egypt with the baby and his mother," the angel said, "and stay there until I tell you to return, for King Herod is going to try to kill the child." That same night he left for Egypt with Mary and the baby, and stayed there until King Herod's death. This fulfilled the prophet's prediction, "I have called my Son from Egypt."

herod was furious when he learned that the astrologers had disobeyed him. Sending soldiers to Bethlehem, he ordered them to kill every baby boy two years old and under, both in the town and on the nearby farms, for the astrologers had told him the star first appeared to them two years before.

This brutal action of Herod's fulfilled the prophecy of Jeremiah,

> *"Screams of anguish come from Ramah,*
> *Weeping unrestrained;*
> *Rachel weeping for her children,*
> *Uncomforted—*
> *For they are dead."*

When Herod died, an angel of the Lord appeared in a dream to Joseph in Egypt, and told him, "Get up and take the baby and his mother back to Israel, for those who were trying to kill the child are dead."

So he returned immediately to Israel with Jesus and his mother.

But on the way he was frightened to learn that the new king was Herod's son, Archelaus. Then, in another dream, he was warned not to go to Judea, so they went to Galilee instead, and lived in Nazareth. This fulfilled the prediction of the prophets concerning the Messiah, "He shall be called a Nazarene."

*t*here the child became a strong, robust lad,
and was known for wisdom beyond his years;
and God poured out his blessings on him.

He shall be as the light of the
*   morning*
A cloudless sunrise
When the tender grass
Springs forth upon the earth
As sunshine after rain.

When Jesus was twelve years old he accompanied his parents to Jerusalem for the annual Passover Festival, which they attended each year. After the celebration was over they started home to Nazareth, but Jesus stayed behind in Jerusalem. His parents didn't miss him the first day, for they assumed he was with friends among the other travelers. But when he didn't show up that evening, they started to look for him among their relatives and friends; and when they couldn't find him, they went back to Jerusalem to search for him there.

*t*hree days later they finally discovered him. He was in the Temple, sitting among the teachers of Law, discussing deep questions with them and amazing everyone with his understanding and answers.

The Spirit of the Lord shall rest upon him,
the Spirit of wisdom, understanding, counsel and might,
the Spirit of knowledge and of the fear of the Lord.

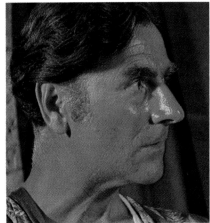

In the book written by the prophet Isaiah, God announced that he would send his Son to earth, and that a special messenger would arrive first to prepare the world for his coming. "This messenger will live out in the barren wilderness," Isaiah said, "and will proclaim that everyone must straighten out his life to be ready for the Lord's arrival."

This messenger was John the Baptist. In the words of Isaiah the prophet, John was "a voice shouting from the barren wilderness, 'Prepare a road for the Lord to travel on! Widen the pathway before him! Level the mountains! Fill up the valleys! Straighten the curves! Smooth out the ruts! And then all mankind shall see the Savior sent from God.'"

Everyone was expecting the Messiah to come soon, and eager to know whether or not John was he. This was the question of the hour and it was discussed everywhere.

John answered the question by saying, "I baptize only with water; but someone is coming soon who has far higher authority than mine; in fact, I am not even worthy of being his slave. He will baptize you with fire—with the Holy Spirit. He will separate chaff from grain, and burn up the chaff with eternal fire and store away the grain."

Then one day, after the crowds had been baptized, Jesus himself was baptized; and as he was praying, the heavens opened, and the Holy Spirit in the form of a dove settled upon him, and a voice from heaven said, "You are my much loved Son, yes, my delight."

John pointed him out to the people, telling the crowds, "This is the one I was talking about when I said, 'Someone is coming who is greater by far than I am—for he existed long before I did!' " We have all benefited from the rich blessings he brought to us—blessing upon blessing heaped upon us! For Moses gave us only the Law with its rigid demands and merciless justice, while Jesus Christ brought us loving forgiveness as well.

*t*hen Jesus was led out into the wilderness by the Holy Spirit, to be tempted there by Satan. For forty days and forty nights he ate nothing and became very hungry.

Then Satan tempted him to get food by changing stones into loaves of bread. "It will prove you are the Son of God," he said. But Jesus told him, "No! For the Scriptures tell us that bread won't feed men's souls: obedience to every word of God is what we need."

Then Satan took him to Jerusalem to the roof of the Temple. "Jump off," he said, "and prove you are the Son of God; for the Scriptures declare, 'God will send his angels to keep you from harm,' . . . they will prevent you from smashing on the rocks below."

Jesus retorted, "It also says not to put the Lord your God to a foolish test!"

Next, Satan took him to the peak of a very high mountain and showed him the nations of the world and all their glory. "I'll give it all to you," he said, "if you will only kneel and worship me."

"Get out of here, Satan," Jesus told him. "The Scriptures say, 'Worship only the Lord God. Obey only him.'" Then Satan went away, and angels came and cared for Jesus.

Even though Jesus was God's Son, he had to learn from experience what it was like to obey, when obeying meant suffering.

Since he himself has now been through suffering and temptation, he knows what it is like when we suffer and are tempted, and he is wonderfully able to help us.

So let us come boldly to the very throne of God and stay there to receive his mercy and to find grace to help us in our times of need.

*t*hen Jesus returned to Galilee, full of the Holy Spirit's power. Soon he became well known throughout all that region for his sermons in the synagogues; everyone praised him.

When he came to the village of Nazareth, his boyhood home, he went as usual to the synagogue on Saturday, and stood up to read the Scriptures.

The book of Isaiah the prophet was handed to him, and he opened it to the place where it says:

"The Spirit of the Lord is upon me; he has appointed me to preach Good News to the poor; he has sent me to heal the brokenhearted and to announce that captives shall be released and the blind shall see, that the downtrodden shall be freed from their oppressors, and that God is ready to give blessings to all who come to him."

He closed the book and handed it back to the attendant and sat down, while everyone in the synagogue gazed at him intently.

Then he added, "These Scriptures came true today!"

Jesus' mother was a guest at a wedding in the village of Cana in Galilee, and Jesus and his disciples were invited too. The wine supply ran out during the festivities.

Six stone waterpots were standing there; they were used for Jewish ceremonial purposes, and held perhaps twenty to thirty gallons each.

Jesus told the servants to fill them to the brim with water. When this was done he said, "Dip some out and take it to the master of ceremonies."

When the master of ceremonies tasted the water that was now wine, not knowing where it had come from (though, of course, the servants did), he called the bridegroom over.

"This is wonderful stuff!" he said. "You're different from most. Usually a host uses the best wine first. But you have kept the best for the last!"

This miracle at Cana in Galilee was Jesus' first public demonstration of his heaven-sent power.

Soon afterwards he went out into the mountains to pray, and prayed all night. At daybreak he called together his followers and chose twelve of them to be the inner circle of his disciples. (They were appointed as his "apostles," or "missionaries.") Here are their names:

Simon (he also called him Peter),
Andrew (Simon's brother),
James,
John,
Philip,
Bartholomew,
Matthew,
Thomas,
James (the son of Alphaeus),
Simon (a member of the Zealots, a subversive political party),
Judas (son of James),
Judas Iscariot (who later betrayed him).

One day as the crowds were gathering, he went up the hillside with his disciples and sat down and taught them there.

"Humble men are very fortunate!" he told them, "for the Kingdom of Heaven is given to them. Those who mourn are fortunate for they shall be comforted. The meek and lowly are fortunate for the whole wide world belongs to them.

"Happy are those who long to be just and good, for they shall be completely satisfied. Happy are the kind and merciful, for they shall be shown mercy. Happy are those whose hearts are pure, for they shall see God. Happy are those who strive for peace—they shall be called the sons of God. Happy are those who are persecuted because they are good, for the Kingdom of Heaven is theirs.

"When you are reviled and persecuted and lied about because you are my followers—wonderful! Be happy about it. Be very glad. For a tremendous reward awaits you up in heaven."

a huge crowd, many of them pilgrims on their way to Jerusalem for the annual Passover celebration, were following him wherever he went, to watch him heal the sick. So when Jesus went up into the hills and sat down with his disciples around him, he soon saw a great multitude of people climbing the hill, looking for him.

Turning to Philip he asked, "Philip, where can we buy bread to feed all these people?" (He was testing Philip, for he already knew what he was going to do.)

Philip replied, "It would take a fortune to begin to do it!"

hen Andrew, Simon Peter's brother, spoke up. "There's a youngster here with five barley loaves and a couple of fish! But what good is that with all this mob?"

"Tell everyone to sit down," Jesus ordered. And all of them—the approximate count of the men only was 5000—sat down on the grassy slopes. Then Jesus took the loaves and gave thanks to God and passed them out to the people. Afterwards he did the same with the fish. And everyone ate until full!

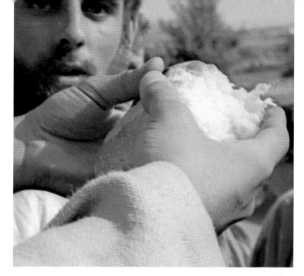

"Now gather the scraps," Jesus told his disciples, "so that nothing is wasted." And twelve baskets were filled with the leftovers!

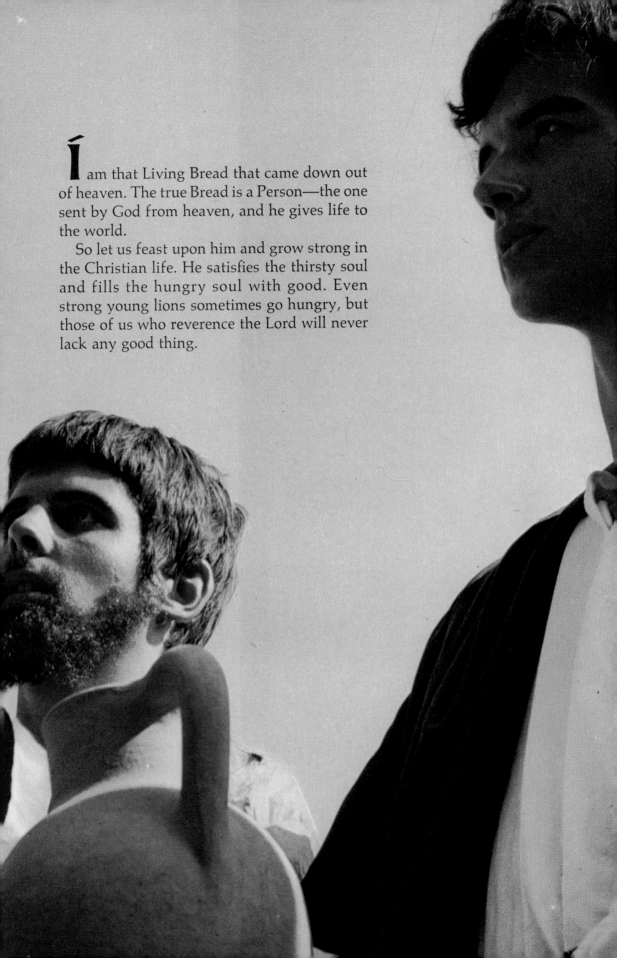

Í am that Living Bread that came down out of heaven. The true Bread is a Person—the one sent by God from heaven, and he gives life to the world.

So let us feast upon him and grow strong in the Christian life. He satisfies the thirsty soul and fills the hungry soul with good. Even strong young lions sometimes go hungry, but those of us who reverence the Lord will never lack any good thing.

*t*he Jewish leaders and Pharisees brought a woman caught in adultery and placed her out in the front of the staring crowd.

"Teacher," they said to Jesus, "this woman was caught in the very act of adultery. Moses' law says to kill her. What about it?"

They were trying to trap him into saying something they could use against him, but Jesus stooped down and wrote in the dust with his finger. They kept demanding an answer, so he stood up again and said, "All right, hurl the stones at her until she dies. But only he who never sinned may throw the first!" Then he stooped down again and wrote some more in the dust.

And the Jewish leaders slipped away one by one, beginning with the eldest, until only Jesus was left in front of the crowd with the woman.

Then Jesus stood up again, and said to her, "Where are your accusers? Didn't even one of them condemn you?"

"No, sir," she said.

And Jesus said, "Neither do I. Go and sin no more."

He forgives all my sins.
He heals me. He ransoms me from hell.
He surrounds me with loving kindness and tender mercies.
He gives justice
to all who are treated unfairly.

What can we ever say to such wonderful things as these?
If God is on our side, who can ever be against us?
Since he did not spare even his own Son for us
but gave him up for us all,
won't he also surely give us everything else?
Everything you need and more,
so that there will not only be enough
for your own needs,
but plenty left over to give joyfully to others.

*a*s he was walking along, he saw a man blind from birth. "Master," his disciples asked him, "why was this man born blind? Was it a result of his own sins or those of his parents?"

"Neither," Jesus answered. "But to demonstrate the power of God. All of us must quickly carry out the tasks assigned us by the one who sent me, for there is little time left before the night falls and all work comes to an end. But while I am still here in the world, I give it my light."

Then he spat on the ground and made mud from the spittle and smoothed the mud over the blind man's eyes, and told him, "Go and wash in the Pool of Siloam."

So the man went where he was sent and washed and came back seeing!

His neighbors and others who knew him as a blind beggar asked each other, "Is this the same fellow—that beggar?" Some said yes, and some said no. "It can't be the same man," they thought, "but he surely looks like him."

And the beggar said, "I *am* the same man."

Then they asked him how in the world he could see. What had happened? And he told them, "A man they call Jesus made mud and smoothed it over my eyes and told me to go to the Pool of Siloam and wash off the mud. I did, and I can see!"

*t*he Jewish leaders wouldn't believe he had been blind, until they called in his parents and asked them, "Is this your son? Was he born blind? If so, how can he see?"

His parents replied, "We know this is our son and that he was born blind, but we don't know what happened to make him see, or who did it. He is old enough to speak for himself. Ask him."

So for the second time they called in the man who had been blind and told him, "Give the glory to God, not to Jesus, for we know Jesus is an evil person."

"I don't know whether he is good or bad," the man replied, "but I know this: I was blind, and now I see!"

Jesus began to speak plainly to his disciples about going to Jerusalem, and what would happen to him there—that he would suffer at the hands of the Jewish leaders, that he would be killed, and that three days later he would be raised to life again.

Then Jesus said to his disciples, "You must put aside your own pleasures and shoulder your cross, and follow me closely. If you insist on saving your life, you will lose it. Only those who throw away their lives for my sake and for the sake of the Good News will ever know what it means to really live.

"What profit is there if you gain the whole world—and lose eternal life? What can be compared with the value of eternal life?"

Heaven can be entered only through the narrow gate!
The highway to hell is broad,
and its gate is wide enough for
all the multitudes who choose its easy way.
But the Gateway to Life is small,
and the road is narrow, and only a few ever find it.

a Jewish religious leader asked him this question: "Good sir, what shall I do to get to heaven?"

"Do you realize what you are saying when you call me 'good'?" Jesus asked him. "Only God is truly good, and no one else.

"But as to your question, you know what the ten commandments say—don't commit adultery, don't murder, don't steal, don't lie, honor your parents and so on." The man replied, "I've obeyed every one of these laws since I was a small child."

"There is still one thing you lack," Jesus said. "Sell all you have and give the money to the poor—it will become treasure for you in heaven—and come, follow me."

But when the man heard this he went sadly away, for he was very rich.

Jesus watched him go, and then said to his disciples, "How hard it is for the rich to enter the Kingdom of God!"

And Peter said, "We have left our homes and followed you."

"Yes," Jesus replied, "and everyone who has done as you have, leaving home, wife, brothers, parents, or children for the sake of the Kingdom of God, will be repaid many times over now, as well as receiving eternal life in the world to come."

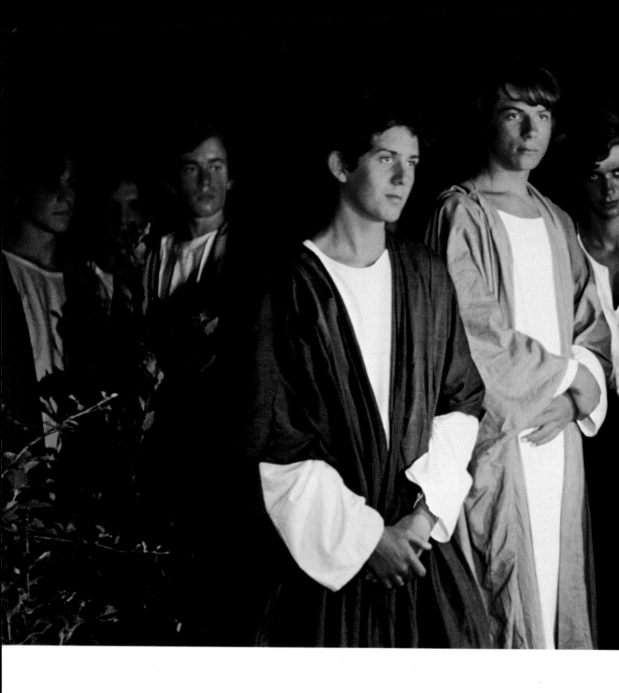

*g*athering the Twelve around him he told them, "As you know, we are going to Jerusalem. And when we get there, all the predictions of the ancient prophets concerning me will come true. I, the Messiah, will be arrested and taken before the chief priests and the Jewish leaders, who will sentence me to die and hand me over to the Romans to be killed. They will mock me and spit on me and flog me with their whips and kill me; but after three days I will come back to life again."

Jesus went on towards Jerusalem, walking along ahead of his disciples. As they came to the towns of Bethphage and Bethany, on the Mount of Olives, he sent two disciples ahead, with instructions to go to the next village, and as they entered they were to look for a donkey tied beside the road. It would be a colt, not yet broken for riding.

"Untie him," Jesus said, "and bring him here. And if anyone asks you what you are doing, just say, 'The Lord needs him.' "

They found the colt as Jesus said, and sure enough, as they were untying it, the owners demanded an explanation.

"What are you doing?" they asked. "Why are you untying our colt?"

And the disciples simply replied, "The Lord needs him." So they brought the colt to Jesus and threw some of their clothing across its back for Jesus to sit on.

*t*hen the crowds spread out their robes along the road ahead of him, and as they reached the place where the road started down from the Mount of Olives, the whole procession began to shout and sing as they walked along, praising God for all the wonderful miracles Jesus had done.

Rejoice greatly, O my people! Shout with joy! For look—your King is coming! He is the Righteous One, the Victor! Yet he is lowly, riding on a donkey's colt!

> *Arm yourself, O mighty One,*
> *So glorious, so majestic!*
> *And in your majesty*
> *Go on to victory,*
> *Defending truth, humility, and justice.*
> *Go forth to awe-inspiring deeds.*

The news that Jesus was on the way to Jerusalem swept through the city, and a huge crowd of Passover visitors took palm branches and went down the road to meet him, shouting, "The Savior! God bless the King of Israel! Hail to God's Ambassador!"

On the first day of the Passover, the day the lambs were sacrificed, his disciples asked him where he wanted to go to eat the traditional Passover supper. He sent two of them into Jerusalem to make the arrangements.

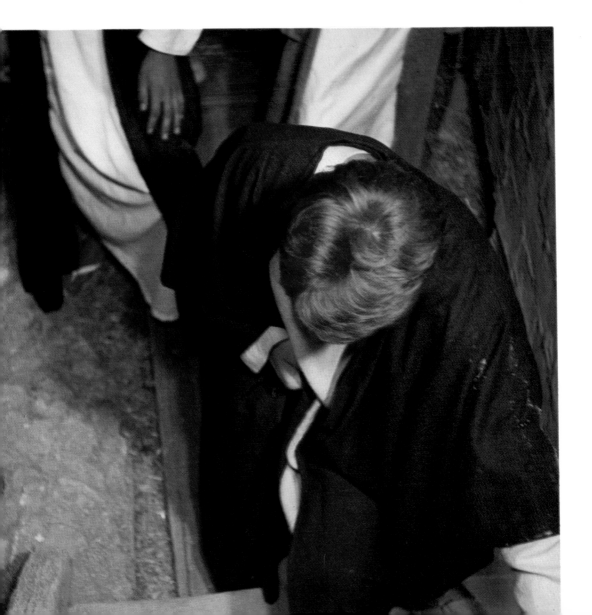

"As you are walking along," he told them, "you will see a man coming towards you carrying a pot of water. Follow him. At the house he enters, tell the man in charge, 'Our Master sent us to see the room you have ready for us, where we will eat the Passover supper this evening!' He will take you upstairs to a large room all set up. Prepare our supper there."

So the two disciples went on ahead into the city and found everything as Jesus had said, and prepared the Passover.

In the evening Jesus arrived with the other disciples. All sat down together at the table; and he said, "I have looked forward to this hour with deep longing, anxious to eat this Passover meal with you before my suffering begins."

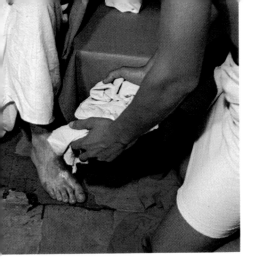

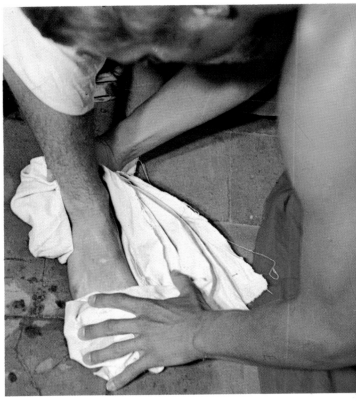

esus knew on the evening of Passover Day that it would be his last night on earth before returning to his Father. During supper the devil had already suggested to Judas Iscariot, Simon's son, that this was the night to carry out his plan to betray Jesus. Jesus knew that the Father had given him everything and that he had come from God and would return to God. And how he loved his disciples! So he got up from the supper table, took off his robe, wrapped a towel around his loins, poured water into a basin, and began to wash the disciples' feet and to wipe them with the towel he had around him.

After washing their feet, he put on his robe again and sat down.

And as they were sitting around the table eating, Jesus said, "I solemnly declare that one of you will betray me, one of you who is here eating with me."

The disciples looked at each other, wondering whom he could mean. Since [John] was sitting next to Jesus at the table, being his closest friend, Simon Peter motioned to [him] to ask him who it was who would do this terrible deed.

So [he] turned and asked him, "Lord, who is it?"

he told [him], "It is the one I honor by giving the bread dipped in the sauce." And when he had dipped it, he gave it to Judas, son of Simon Iscariot.

as soon as Judas had eaten it, Satan entered into him. Then Jesus told him, "Hurry—do it now." Judas left at once, going out into the night.

*a*s soon as Judas left the room, Jesus said, "My time has come; the glory of God will soon surround me—and God shall receive great praise because of all that happens to me. And God shall give me his own glory, and this so very soon. I am leaving you with a gift— peace of mind and heart! And the peace I give isn't fragile like the peace the world gives. So don't be troubled or afraid. I am going away but I will come back to you again.

"I don't have much more time to talk to you, for the evil prince of this world approaches. He has no power over me, but I will freely do what the Father requires of me so that the world will know that I love the Father. Come, let's be going."

Then they sang a hymn and went out to the Mount of Olives.

Jesus brought them to a garden grove, Gethsemane, and told them to sit down and wait while he went ahead to pray. He took Peter with him and Zebedee's two sons James and John, and began to be filled with anguish and despair.

Then he told them, "My soul is crushed with horror and sadness to the point of death . . . stay here . . . stay awake with me."

He went forward a little, and fell face downward on the ground, and prayed, "My Father! If it is possible, let this cup be taken away from me. But I want your will, not mine."

*t*hen an angel from heaven appeared and strengthened him, for he was in such agony of spirit that he broke into a sweat of blood, with great drops falling to the ground as he prayed more and more earnestly.

*t*hen he returned to the three disciples and found them asleep. "Peter," he called, "couldn't you even stay awake with me one hour? Keep alert and pray. Otherwise temptation will overpower you. For the spirit indeed is willing, but how weak the body is!"

Again he left them and prayed, "My Father! If this cup cannot go away until I drink it all, your will be done."

He returned to them again and found them sleeping, for their eyes were heavy, so he went back to prayer the third time, saying the same things again.

Then he came to the disciples and said, "Sleep on now and take your rest . . . but no! The time has come! I am betrayed into the hands of evil men! Up! Let's be going! Look! Here comes the man who is betraying me!"

Judas, the betrayer, knew this place, for Jesus had gone there many times with his disciples. The chief priests and Pharisees had given Judas a squad of soldiers and police to accompany him. Now, with blazing torches, lanterns and weapons, they arrived at the olive grove. Jesus fully realized all that was going to happen to him. Stepping forward to meet them he asked,

"Whom are you looking for?"

"Jesus of Nazareth," they replied.

"I am he," Jesus said.

Judas had told them, "You will know which one to arrest when I go over and greet him. Then you can take him easily." So as soon as they arrived he walked up to Jesus. "Master!" he exclaimed, and embraced him. Then the mob arrested Jesus and held him fast.

Jesus addressed the chief priests and captains of the Temple guards and the religious leaders who headed the mob. "This is your moment—the time when Satan's power reigns supreme!"

Lord, how you have helped me before! You took me safely from my mother's womb and brought me through the years of infancy. I have depended upon you since birth; you have always been my God. Don't leave me now, for trouble is near and no one else can possibly help. O Lord, don't stay away. O God my Strength, hurry to my aid.

$t$hen the mob led him to the home of Caiaphas the High Priest, where all the Jewish leaders were gathering.

The High Priest said to him, "I demand in the name of the living God that you tell us whether you claim to be the Messiah, the Son of God."

"Yes," Jesus said, "I am. And in the future you will see me, the Messiah, sitting at the right hand of God and returning on the clouds of heaven."

Then the High Priest tore at his clothing, shouting, "Blasphemy! What need have we for other witnesses? You have all heard him say it! What is your verdict?"

They shouted, "Death!—Death!—Death!"

*e*arly the next morning at daybreak the Jewish Supreme Court assembled, including the chief priests and all the top religious authorities of the nation. Jesus was led before this Council, and instructed to state whether or not he claimed to be the Messiah.

He replied, "Yes, I am."

Then the entire Council took Jesus over to Pilate, the governor.

"We want him crucified," they demanded, "and your approval is required."

Pilate called together the chief priests and other Jewish leaders, along with the people, and announced his verdict:

"You brought this man to me, accusing him of leading a revolt against the Roman government. I have examined him thoroughly on this point and find him innocent."

And they shouted, "Crucify him!"

"Why?" Pilate demanded. "What has he done wrong?"

But they kept shouting, "Crucify! Crucify!"

"Why? What crime has he committed? I have found no reason to sentence him to death. I will therefore scourge him and let him go." But they shouted louder and louder for Jesus' death. So Pilate sentenced Jesus to die as they demanded.

Pilate laid open Jesus' back with a leaded whip, and the soldiers made a crown of thorns and placed it on his head and robed him in royal purple.

"Hail, King of the Jews!" they mocked, and struck him with their fists.

Pilate went outside again and said to the Jews, "I am going to bring him out to you now, but understand clearly that I find him *not guilty.*"

Jesus came out wearing the crown of thorns and the purple robe. And Pilate said, "Behold the man!" At sight of him the chief priests and Jewish officials began yelling, "Crucify! Crucify!"

Then Pilate gave Jesus to them to be crucified.

So they had him at last, and he was taken out of the city, carrying his cross to the place known as "The Skull," in Hebrew, "Golgotha."

there they crucified him and two others with him, one on either side, with Jesus between them.

Then they sat around and watched him as he hung there.

"Father, forgive these people," Jesus said, "for they don't know what they are doing."

The people passing by hurled abuse, shaking their heads at him. And the chief priests and Jewish leaders also mocked him. "He saved others," they scoffed, "but he can't save himself!"

y strength has drained away like water, and all my bones are out of joint. My heart melts like wax; my strength has dried up like sunbaked clay; my tongue sticks to my mouth. The enemy, this gang of evil men, circles me like a pack of dogs; they have pierced my hands and feet. Everyone who sees me mocks and sneers and shrugs.

That afternoon, the whole earth was covered with darkness for three hours, from noon until three o'clock. About three o'clock, Jesus shouted, "Eli, Eli, lama sabachthani," which means, "My God, my God, why have you forsaken me?"

Jesus knew that everything was now finished, and to fulfill the Scriptures said, "I'm thirsty." A jar of sour wine was sitting there, so a sponge was soaked in it and put on a hyssop branch and held up to his lips. When Jesus had tasted it, he said, "It is finished." Then Jesus shouted, "Father, I commit my spirit to you," and with those words he died.

When the captain of the Roman military unit handling the executions saw what had happened, he was stricken with awe before God and said, "Surely this man was innocent."

And when the crowd that came to see the crucifixion saw that Jesus was dead, they went home in deep sorrow. And many women who had come down from Galilee with Jesus to care for him were watching from a distance. Among them were Mary Magdalene and Mary the mother of James and Joseph, and the mother of James and John (the sons of Zebedee).

ⲱhen evening came, a rich man from Arimathea named Joseph, one of Jesus' followers, went to Pilate and asked for Jesus' body. And Pilate issued an order to release it to him. Joseph took the body and wrapped it in a clean linen cloth, and placed it in his own new rock-hewn tomb, and rolled a great stone across the entrance as he left. Both Mary Magdalene and the other Mary were sitting nearby watching.

The next day—at the close of the first day of the Passover ceremonies—the chief priests and Pharisees went to Pilate, and told him, "Sir, that liar once said, 'After three days I will come back to life again.' So we request an order from you sealing the tomb until the third day, to prevent his disciples from coming and stealing his body and then telling everyone he came back to life! If that happens we'll be worse off than we were at first."

"Use your own Temple police," Pilate told them. "They can guard it safely enough."

So they sealed the stone and posted guards to protect it from intrusion.

*e*arly on Sunday morning, as the new day was dawning, Mary Magdalene and the other Mary went out to the tomb. On the way they were discussing how they could ever roll aside the huge stone from the entrance. But when they arrived they looked up and saw that the stone—a very heavy one—was already moved away and the entrance was open! So they went in—but the Lord Jesus' body was gone.

They stood there puzzled, trying to think what could have happened to it. Suddenly two men appeared before them, clothed in shining robes so bright their eyes were dazzled. The women were terrified and bowed low before them.

Then the men asked, "Why are you looking in a tomb for someone who is alive? He isn't here! He has come back to life again! Don't you remember what he told you back in Galilee—that the Messiah must be betrayed into the power of evil men and be crucified and that he would rise again the third day?"

The women fled from the tomb, trembling and bewildered, too frightened to talk.

𝓶ary Magdalene ran and found Simon Peter and John and said, "They have taken the Lord's body out of the tomb, and I don't know where they have put him!"

Simon Peter and John ran to the tomb to see; John outran Peter and got there first, and stooped and looked in and saw the linen cloth lying there, but he didn't go in. Then Simon Peter arrived and went on inside. He also noticed the cloth lying there, while the swath that had covered Jesus' head was rolled up in a bundle and was lying at the side. Then John went in too, and saw, and believed.

Simon Peter and John went on home, and by that time Mary had returned to the tomb and was standing outside crying.

She glanced over her shoulder and saw someone standing behind her. It was Jesus, but she didn't recognize him!

"Why are you crying?" he asked her. "Whom are you looking for?"

She thought he was the gardener. "Sir," she said, "if you have taken him away, tell me where you have put him, and I will go and get him."

"Mary!" Jesus said. She turned toward him.

"Master!" she exclaimed.

"Don't touch me," he cautioned, "for I haven't yet ascended to the Father. But go find my brothers and tell them that I ascend to my Father and your Father, my God and your God."

She found the disciples wet-eyed with grief and exclaimed that she had seen Jesus, and he was alive! But they didn't believe her!

That evening the disciples were meeting behind locked doors, in fear of the Jewish leaders, when suddenly Jesus was standing there among them! After greeting them, he showed them his hands and side. And how wonderful was their joy as they saw their Lord!

One of the disciples, Thomas "The Twin," was not there at the time with the others. When they kept telling him, "We have seen the Lord," he replied, "I won't believe it unless I see the nail wounds in his hands—and put my fingers into them—and place my hand into his side."

*e*ight days later the disciples were together again, and this time Thomas was with them. The doors were locked; but suddenly, as before, Jesus was standing among them and greeting them. Then he said to Thomas, "Put your finger into my hands. Put your hand into my side. Don't be faithless any longer. Believe!"

"My Lord and my God!" Thomas said.

It was not long afterwards that he rose into the sky and disappeared into a cloud, leaving them staring after him. As they were straining their eyes for another glimpse, suddenly two white-robed men were standing there among them, and said, "Men of Galilee, why are you standing here staring at the sky? Jesus has gone away to heaven, and some day, just as he went, he will return!"

Jesus' disciples saw him do many other miracles besides the ones told about in this book, but these are recorded so that you will believe that he is the Messiah, the Son of God, and that believing in him you will have life. And I suppose that if all the other events in Jesus' life were written, the whole world could hardly contain the books!

The First and Last, the Living One who died,
who is now alive forevermore.
He is robed in majesty and strength.
The world is his throne.
His power is incredible.
O Lord, you have reigned from prehistoric times,
from the everlasting past.
Yours is the mighty power and glory
and victory and majesty.